I STAND A[LONE]

Inspirational Meditations

Rev. Eugene L. Neville

I Stand Amazed
All Rights Reserved.
Copyright © 2020 Rev. Eugene L. Neville
v5.0

This is a work of fiction. The events and characters described herein are imaginary and are not intended to refer to specific places or living persons. The opinions expressed in this manuscript are solely the opinions of the author and do not represent the opinions or thoughts of the publisher. The author has represented and warranted full ownership and/or legal right to publish all the materials in this book.

This book may not be reproduced, transmitted, or stored in whole or in part by any means, including graphic, electronic, or mechanical without the express written consent of the publisher except in the case of brief quotations embodied in critical articles and reviews.

Outskirts Press, Inc.
http://www.outskirtspress.com

ISBN: 978-1-9772-1746-2

Cover Photo © 2020 Rev. Eugene L. Neville. All rights reserved - used with permission.

Outskirts Press and the "OP" logo are trademarks belonging to Outskirts Press, Inc.

PRINTED IN THE UNITED STATES OF AMERICA

DEDICATION

I dedicate this book in memory of my parents, David and Evelyn Neville, and my father and mother-in-law, Carl and Johnnie Ellis, for the years of loving kindness, and support they showered upon me throughout the years. I will forever, be grateful for the rich legacy of faith, and the invaluable examples of love they set before me. I am confident; they are seated before the presence of Almighty God.

ACKNOWLEDGEMENT

I am greatly pleased to have included in this book, several of the magnificent pieces of art, painted by my wife Ruth. Her artwork brings to each page a higher level of inspiration. Moreover, it also has been my honor and privilege, to have my sister, Mrs. Jeanette Catherwood, and my very special friend, Mrs. Phyllis Brown, assist me on the early editing of this book. Their contributions were extremely helpful. I know that I would not have been able to complete this work without their insightful analysis, and editorial skills, which were invaluable to me. Thank you!

O Lord, my God,
When I observe the majestic beauty of the universe,
Which Thou, alone created.
The billions of solar systems and galaxies,
The glorious radiance of our sun and moon,
The synchronistic connectivity of Jesus Christ in our lives,
Emanating the effulgence of Thy love and glory.
Like the sages of antiquity,
I Stand Amazed!

CONTENTS

In The Palms of Jesus	1
The Loudest Continuous Sounds in All of the Creation	2
The Long Corridor	4
Womb Conversations	6
God Loves You	7
Dance! Dance! Dance!	8
When I Grow Up	9
What Did I Get Myself Into	11
Don't Forget to Remember	14
The Envy of Solomon	16
Behind the Frosted Glass	18
After a Great Fall	21
But I Still Am	25
A Wonderful Change Has Come Over Me	28
Peek-A-Boo - I See You	30
All I Want for Christmas Is…	36
The Magnificence of a Mothers Love	39
How Did Mama Know?	42
I Can Still Hear Mama Say	50
My Amazing Daughter	54
All Because of My Daughter	57
Who Needs Friends Like These?	59
All Because of a Tree!	61
If Trees Could Talk	64
Life Is Like a Vapor	69
If I Was Created as an Eye	70
The Gifts of God	73
We Cry Abba, Father	74
Mission Impossible	77
The Shaking of Foundations	79
Eagles Do Fall	82
Lord, I Don't Want to Go There	87

Don't Give Up Now!	89
My Life Without You	94
So You Think It No Longer Matters	96
Who Really Cares?	101
Amber-Quocious Friends	103
The Healing Corridors of Faith	105
Hallelujah! I Can See!	107
Lord, Something Is Missing	108
Joy Where Are You hiding?	111
The Agony of Joy	112
The Unmatachable Wonder	115
The Wonder ~ One Can Only Imagine	121
The Highest Place of Praise and Worship	125
I Stand Amazed	134

IN THE PALMS OF JESUS

In the palms of Jesus,
Children are safe.
Children can find joy playing.
Children can laugh and sing.
Children can accept each other's differences.

In the palms of Jesus,
Children are deeply loved.
Children are divinely protected.
Children live their life with hope.
Children are at peace with Almighty God.

THE LOUDEST CONTINUOUS SOUNDS IN ALL OF THE CREATION

The loudest continuous sounds in all of the creation,
Did not come from the eruption of the Krakatoa volcano in 1883.
Nor did the loudest continuous sounds in all of the creation
Come from the majestic birth of new stars in the solar system.
It did not come from Quasars, which are the birthplace of galaxies,
The place of massive collisions of thousands of galaxies
being transformed into awe-inspiring, stellar super galaxies.

It did not come from the implosion or subsequent explosion of super dwarf stars.
It did not even come from the unimaginable sounds
Emitted by the uncountable, supermassive, black holes
That meander the depths of space,
Nothing escaping its gravitational pull.

The loudest continuous sounds in all of the creation,
Come from the least expected place.
A place of serenity, a place of peace, an idyllic place of perfection.
The loudest continuous sounds in all of the creation,
Come from around the throne of Almighty God!

The moment when **anyone**, repents of their sins, and
Accepts Jesus Christ as the Lord of their life.
That moment, thousands upon thousands, and tens of thousands of thousands,
An innumerable number of angels, begin to rejoice,
And shout praises throughout Heaven
To Jesus Christ, the Lamb of God,
And to God, our Heavenly Father.

Jesus said, *"I tell you that in the same way*
there will be more rejoicing in heaven
over one sinner who repents
than over ninety-nine righteous persons
who do not need to repent".

Every moment of time on this special planet, called Earth,
At least one repentant person, who once was lost, but now is saved!

Heaven is that place,
Where the loudest continuous sounds of praise can be heard!

THE LONG CORRIDOR

Wow! My own space!
I can run up and down the hallway all day long.
Here, nobody will tell me to be still.
I can kick my soccer ball into the next room, no one will be there to stop me.
I can shout as loud as I can, the only voice I will hear is my own echo.
This place is awesome!

How did I get in here?
What did I do wrong to deserve this?
What's with all these steps?
How do I get out of here?
What's behind that strange darkness?
Is that the end of the corridor?

Why am I here?
Where are those effervescent lights coming from?
Is the light source real or artificial?
Are these steps descending or ascending?
What do the etchings in the arches mean?
Why is this corridor so long?
Is stepping into that strange darkness the only
Safe way out?

This place is so different.
The path is over laid with a beautiful long red carpet.
The walls are brilliant and elegant.
The arches are fantastic!

My path is now much clearer.
I am now closer to the strange darkness.
I am not afraid. I feel so peaceful.

Wow! It is so amazing!
Standing here in the midst of this Strange Light
It is glorious, majestic, and inexplicably beautiful!

The Lord is my Shepherd.
Even though I may have to continue walking through
This Long Corridor
I will fear no evil because now I can clearly see
God has always been in here with me!

WOMB CONVERSATIONS

Who are you?
How did you get in here with me?
What is that?
That's mine!
I was here first!
Are you gonna drink all that by yourself?
Stop moving so much.
It's time for you to get out of here.
No you get out!
Boy, get back in here!
Get back in here!
What's that on your finger?
I want one too, move out of the way.
Oh! Oh! Oh!

Who are you?
I don't know!
I don't know?
That's mine too!
No you were not, I was!
Yup. It's really good too!
You stop kicking me.
No, you get out!
Girl, I'm out of here!
Somethings screaming!
Pull, pull me harder!
I don't know.
You'll be sorry!
She's finally gone.
Peace at last.
It's all mine!
Oh! Oh! Oh!
I'm out too!
I'm freezing!

GOD LOVES YOU

You are special!
You are beautiful!
You are kind!
You are smart!
You are good!
You are creative!
You are loveable!
You are blessed!
You will be awesome!
You will be phenomenal!
You will succeed!
You are God's child!

*Jesus said, "Let the little children come to me,
and do not hinder them,
for the kingdom of heaven belongs to such as these."*
Matthew 19:14

DANCE! DANCE! DANCE!

I dance to the glory of God!
There is a beautiful feeling of love
Flowing throughout my entire body
Which ignites a passion deep within my soul
Inspiring me to
Dance… Dance… Dance.
The passion of love
Was graciously placed inside of me
Still being inside my mother's womb.
I sense this presence to be
One of the creative gifts
God has designed for me to share.
Therefore, I will
Dance! Dance! Dance!
Always to the glory of God.

WHEN I GROW UP

The dreams of a child are precious
they express the inner thought and aspirations
endowed upon them by Almighty God.

When I grow up,
I would like to become a heart surgeon
to heal people of their hearts major problems
so they can live a better life

I think when I grow up, I might like to become a lawyer
I think I would be able to help kids
who made wrong choices
get another chance to do things right

Maybe, when I grow up,
I might like to become a schoolteacher
to help kids aspire higher
to reach all of their creative potentials

Maybe when I grow up,
I could become an astronaut
to travel deep space
and go where no one has gone before

When I grow up,
I would like to become like Jesus
to love and care about everyone
Like He loves and takes care of me

Lord, during these scary times
I just would like to have the chance
to live long enough to say
I have grown up!

WHAT DID I GET MYSELF INTO

The heights of great people reached and kept
Was not attained by sudden flight
But they while their companions slept
We're toiling upward throughout the night
                    Henry Wadsworth Longfellow

Lord, what did I get myself into?
I am almost going out of my mind.
I am rising up early in the morning,
Before the rising of the sun!
I am not going to bed, before the dawning of a new day.
Lord, what did I get myself into?

I am rushing off from one classroom to the other, all day long!
I am cramming my mind with new concepts, new philosophies, and ideologies.
A new language, new terms, new people, new everything!
Lord, what did I get myself into?

I am sitting under some professors who are talking way over my head.
And others who are constantly putting me to sleep,
Because they are boring.
Every day I have exams to take, and papers to write.
Some professors even expect me,

To read, and learn the content,
Of all their assigned readings, within a week!
Lord, what did I get myself into?

Lord, for all of the money my mother is paying,
The dorm is too noisy!
The room is too small!
The food is horrible!
Lord, what did I get myself into?

I am not sure if it is worth the price.
I am not sleeping peacefully!
I am not eating properly!
Although I am attending all of my classes faithfully,
I am studying diligently, trying my best.
However, I am just narrowly passing all of my courses!

I am still wondering,
What did I get myself into?
If I graduate, will I find an adequate job?
If I graduate, will I be able to attend graduate school?
If I graduate, will I be able to pursue my career goals?
If I graduate, will I be able to pay off these astronomical student loans?
Lord, what did I get myself into?
Was it worth the price I had to pay?
Wow!

I can hardly believe how quickly those 4 years had passed.
I have completed all of my course requirements.
I am dressed in my college graduation regalia.
I am now holding in my hands,
My college degree!
I am so amazed!
I have graduated!
It all has been worth the trials, tests, and tribulations.
Thank you, Lord!
I am ready to face the new challenges,
You placed before me,
That will help me reach the glorious destiny,
You prearranged for my life.

The Lord meticulously prearranges all of the steps of a good person,
The Lord will withhold no good thing from those who Love and trust Him.

DON'T FORGET TO REMEMBER

Has anybody seen my glasses?
Where did I put those keys?
What did I come into this room for?
What day is today?
Where in the world did I park my car?
What's your name again?
Sometimes, I just can't seem to remember anything!
Lord, sometimes I may forget where I placed things
Sometimes I often forget how to get to places
Sometimes I forget how to spell words
Sometimes I even forget how to prepare my favorite recipes
Sometimes I may even forget my family member's name
Sometimes I might even forget how important and special they are to me
Lord, there could even come a day when I might forget
Where I live and how to get home
How to prepare meals for me
When it is time to go to bed or time to get up
How to count numbers or to identify basic colors
How to dial the telephone or to turn off the television
Lord, there may come a day when I forget those things
However, O Lord. May I never forget who Jesus Christ is
Alternatively, what He has done for me
May I never forget that He loves me!
O God, may I never forget to remember

That Jesus suffered, bled and died on Calvary for me
May I never forget to remember that Jesus Christ is
The Son of the Living God
The Redeemer of the world
The Lilly of the valley
The Rose of Sharon
The Bright and Morning Star
The Way, the Truth and the Life
The Great Physician
The Master of Storms and Seas
The Light of the World
The Prince of Peace
The King of kings and Lord of lords
O God, may I never forget to remember
that at the name of Jesus every knee shall bow,
of those in heaven, and of those on earth,
and of those under the earth,
and that every tongue shall confess
that Jesus Christ is Lord,
to the glory of God the Father.

THE ENVY OF SOLOMON

I say unto you, that Solomon in all his glory was not arrayed like one of these. Luke 12 : 27

King Solomon was a great man of antiquity
Majestically arrayed with a multiplicity of gifts
Providentially endowed by Almighty God
King Solomon was the wisest man of his generation
King Solomon was extended the highest honor
To build the Holy Temple in Israel
In accord with the divine specifications
Articulated by God Himself
King Solomon built many glorious structures that amazed the world
King Solomon acquired everything a man ever desired
King Solomon attended the best universities
Mastered all of the academic courses

The languages, sciences, and the humanities
King Solomon lived in immaculate homes
Which startled the imagination

King Solomon acquired treasuries that
Surpassed the national treasury of most countries
King Solomon enjoyed every human pleasure
Man's heart ever desired
King Solomon was a man
Arrayed with a multiplicity of gifts and talents
However, if he were still alive today
He might be envious of me
Because there is one experience
One majestic gift
One phenomenal treasure
One glorious pleasure
One special blessing
King Solomon never could have or will ever experience
The precious blessing
Of calling you
My Great-Grandchildren!

BEHIND THE FROSTED GLASS

I woke up this morning and everything had changed.
Everything appears to be veiled behind a frosted glass.
This day, everything had changed!
Behind the frosted glass,
I took a slow walk out of doors onto the hard surface
Embedded between soft long green paths on each side.
Behind the veil of the frosted glass,
I could feel warm rays piercing through the transitions
From midnight into day.
I felt each gentle breeze kissing my face
As they quickly passed by.
Behind the frosted glass,
Overhead, I heard the calling of a single crow
As it soared through the air.
Followed later by a cacophony of musical notes
Being sung by a fleet of beautiful birds,
Flying and dancing in the air
As they ascended and descended upon treetops and houses.
Behind the frosted glass,
In the far distance,
I could hear muffled hums
As objects traversed the unseen highways.

Behind the frosted glass,
I stepped onto one of the long green paths.
I felt a mist embrace my feet.
It accompanied me each step of the way home.
Behind the frosted glass,
I felt tender drops of water descend from heaven.
Each drop blessed the crown of my head,
And gently flowed down the sides of my face.
Behind the frosted glass,
I smelt a sweet fragrance
Like a perfectly refined perfume
Saturating the entire environment.
Behind the frosted glass,
I heard a kind word of encouragement
Uttered to me from an unseen stranger.
~ Good morning!
Behind the frosted glass,
Unexpectedly, I heard the loud thrashing of falling objects,
The squealing of gears,
The racing of a loud motor as it slowly passed,
Stopping intermittingly.
I heard familiar sounds of large objects
Being cast to the ground.
The sweet fragrance became odorous fumes
as the vehicle passed along the way.
Behind the frosted glass,
I heard the screeching and slamming of large metal doors.
I could not wait until I arrived at where I had first started.
Once again, I was home.
Behind the frosted glass,
I smelt the aroma of freshly brewed coffee.
I smelt bacon cooking on the stove.
I heard inspirational gospel music
Pulsating in and out of my office.

Something deep inside of me
Would not let me withhold my song of praise!
Thank You, Lord, for blessing me,
Behind the frosted glass of praise!

AFTER A GREAT FALL

Humpty Dumpty had a great fall.
All of the great physicians, politicians, theologians, scientists,
And technologists of his generation, could not figure out,
How to rejoin the shattered and fragmented pieces
Of his life back to wholeness again.
There was no hope for Humpty Dumpty.
His fall was fatal, and eternal.

What about the countless Humpty Dumpties' of our generation,
Who in like manner, have experienced great falls?
Who fell into depression.
Who fell into family discord.
Who fell into financial indebtedness.
Who fell into addictive lifestyles.
Whose fall resulted in more than minor bruises?

Was their fall caused by an unforeseeable accident?
Was their fall caused by making wrong choices?
Was their fall caused by the deliberate slipping away
From the grace of God?
Whatever the cause of their fall,
Was their fall beyond the possibility of restoration?

Is there anyone, other than the inept physicians, politicians,
Theologians, scientists, and technologists,
Who has the restorative ability, and power, to reconstruct
The shattered and fragmented pieces of their lives?

Yes there is!
Jesus Christ can restore shattered and fragmented lives!
Jesus Christ is the Expert Restorer!
There is salvation in no one else!
God has given no other name under heaven,
Who can save and restore us. Acts 4:12

Jesus is the Son of the living God.
Jesus is the Expert Restorer.
He can restore and heal with only a touch.
He can restore and heal by only speaking a word.
Throughout the annuals of time,
An inestimable number of people,
Were restored and healed to newness of life,
By one drop of his precious blood.

By the power of his spoken word,
Blind people received their sight again.
Lame and paralyzed people, walked again.
Emotional disturbed people, reclaim their mind again.
Socially outcast were restored to their communities again.
Even the dead were raised to life,
Moreover, were reunited to their family again.

Only Jesus the Christ, has the power and authority
To restore, and to heal, the Humpty Dumpties' of the world.
Like Humpty Dumpty, we all have slipped and fallen.

The great fall of humanity,
Came as a direct result of the incursion of sin.
Sin completely severed the relationship with our Creator.
Moreover, the great fall, left all of humanity,
Without the possibility of saving or restoring ourselves.
The great fall left all of humanity like Humpty Dumpty.
Shattered, fragmented, and estranged from God.
Thereby, without hope.
However, God,
Out of His great love and tender mercy for all of humanity,
By grace, sent his one and only Son, Jesus,
To be the healer, and restorer for all of humanity.
Jesus the Christ, was the only one chosen by God,
Who could make atonement for the sins of the world.
The cost required the sacrifice of his own life.
Jesus paid the full price.
Willingly, he laid down his life at Calvary.

He was wounded for our transgressions,
He was bruised for our iniquities:
The chastisement of our peace was on him;
In addition, with his stripes we are healed.   Isaiah 53:5

Moreover, He died, but on the third day, He arose from the dead,
As the victor, over sin, death and the grave.
With all authority and power in His hands,
He is able to reverse every condition that impacts the lives
Of those who place their faith and hope in Him.
The once shattered and fragmented pieces of their lives,
Are conjoined into wholeness, and holiness.
The Humpty Dumpties' of the world, now become
New creations in Jesus Christ.

All of humanity has fallen,
However, God gives each of us another chance
To make wiser decisions.
The wisest decision is to choose God's gift of grace
Before the second great fall occurs...death.
Without Christ in one's life.
That second fall, made by a personal choice, will be fatal, and without hope.

Humpty Dumpty, there is hope!
You can be made whole and holy again!

BUT I STILL AM

Lord, I am not worthy to come before your holy presence.
My many sins surround me every day.
I feel so ashamed, so worthless, and so afraid.
I don't know where to turn for help, but only to you, Lord.

Lord, I don't wanna be a sinner in my heart… But I still am!
Lord, I don't wanna be a liar, a manipulator or a thief … But I still am!
Lord, I don't wanna be selfish, self-centered or self-righteous … But I still am!
Lord, I don't wanna be unfair, ungrateful or unfaithful … But I still am!
Lord, I don't wanna be a sinner in my heart…But I still am!

Lord, I don't wanna be controlled by prejudice, meanness or evil …But I still am!
Lord, I don't wanna be an addict, an alcoholic or a sexual predator…But I still am!
Lord, I don't wanna live without love, without peace or without hope … But I still am!
Lord, I don't wanna be a sinner in my heart any more…But I still am!

Lord, I don't wanna abuse, mistreat or hurt my family any longer… But I still do!
Lord, I don't wanna live with fear, jealousy or hatred in my heart… But I still am!
Lord I don't wanna get in trouble no more, go to jail or prison …But I still might!
Lord, I don't wanna die in this condition…But I still could!

O wretched man that I am!
Lord, is there any hope for a person like me?
Who can deliver me from my sin sick soul?
Who can heal my wounded spirit, and my troubled mind?
Who can make my life worth living?
Who can help me?
Who can save me?

The prayer God desires is a broken spirit.
God will never reject an honest and repentant heart.
Yes, there is hope for you through Jesus the Christ,
Because of who He is and what He did for the world.

Jesus said **I would**… Because I still am the One who created you, and breathed life and purpose into your life.

Jesus said **I would**… Because I still am the One who has watched over you, and held you safely in the palm of my hand.

Jesus said **I would**… Because I still am the One who will reset all of the defaults of your fragmented life.

Jesus said **I would**… Because I still am the same yesterday, today, and forever.
… Because I still am the Way, the Truth, and the Life.
… Because my mercies are eternal, and my love is everlasting.
… Because I still am the Author and Finisher of all faith.
… Because I still am the Light of the world.
… Because I still am the Resurrection and the Life.

Jesus said **I would**… Because I still am the only One in all of creation who could sacrifice his life to atone for the sins of the entire world.

Jesus said **I would**… Because I still am the only One whose blood can cleanse, heal, deliver, and save all of humanity.

Jesus said **I would**… Because I still am the only One who has conquered the power of sin, death, and the grave.

Jesus said **I would**… Because I still am the only One who is able to present a sinner,

faultless, justified, and holy before the presence of Almighty God.
Jesus said **I would**… Because I still am the only Christ, the Savior of the world!

My son, I love you!
My son, do you want to be whole?
My son, do you want to be saved?
Yes, Jesus! I wanna be whole.
Yes, Jesus, I wanna believe in You with all of my heart.
Yes, Jesus, I wanna be a Christian in my heart.
Yes, Jesus, I wanna live my new life totally committed to You.

For God so loved the world that he gave his one and only Son,
that whoever believes in him shall not perish but have eternal life. John 3:16

A WONDERFUL CHANGE HAS COME OVER ME

Ever since, Jesus Christ found, and saved me,
My life has never been the same.
I have been changed!
The harmful things I used to do,
I don't do them anymore.
The places I used to go,
I don't go there anymore.
The things I used to say,
I don't say them anymore.
The things I used to believe,
I don't believe them anymore.
A wonderful change has come over me.

I have been forgiven of all my sins.
I am now completely whole!
I no longer am lost, and alone.
I no longer am heart broken.
I no longer am angry.
I no longer am afraid of life.
I found in Jesus Christ, a lasting peace of mind.
I found in Jesus Christ, unimaginable joy.

I found in Jesus Christ, the source of pure love.
I found in Jesus Christ, the blessed hope of eternal life.
I found in Jesus Christ,
My Lord, Savior and eternal King.
A wonderful change has come over me!

The real good news is this.
The same wonderful change will come over you,
If you confess with your mouth,
In addition, believe in your heart,
As I did, that Jesus Christ sacrificed his own life,
To rescue us from all of those sin filled things.
Then you will be saved!
In addition, you will exclaim,
A wonderful change has come over me!

PEEK-A-BOO – I SEE YOU

When some of us were little babies
Our parents played a simple game with us
That was passed down through the generations.
They covered their eyes with both hands
Then quickly flashed them open.
With a broad smile on their face they said,
"Peek-a-boo, I see you!"
In response, we would laugh and they would continue.

As the years passed, we might have also been taught
Not to believe everything you see without careful examination.
In addition, everything that glitters is not always pure gold.
Moreover, the grass is not always greener on the other side of the street.
Lastly, beauty is only skin-deep.

Some of us have been blessed by these words of wise counsel.
Today, we all must be careful about the things that we embrace.
We all should seek the ability to discern
The truth from falsehood,
Reality from mythology,
Authentic faith from religious piety,
The sacred from the secular, and
The path of life from the paths of destruction.

There are some things in this world
That we must clearly see and understand for ourselves.
In addition, we must come to know that God does exist.

There are things in the world that should remain sacred.
Although there are things, we cannot see through natural eyesight,
Nevertheless, in actuality, they do exist.

On the other hand, there are many things
That we can visually see with our own eyes.
However, these things are only the creative imagination.
Major companies have commercialized,
Exclusively f or business purposes or self-aggrandizement,
Especially during major religious holidays,
Christmas and Easter.

The real purpose of the occasions,
Is often obscured by creation of fictional animations,
Which overshadows the spiritual reason,
Value and benefits of the season.

One of the most important events
Which undoubtedly has altered
The entire course of human history is
The birth of Jesus Christ,
The Savior of the world.

This sacred, historic event has been obscured
By the over-commercialization of the proverbial Christmas, tree.
In addition, by the numerous Santa Clause mythologies.
For example, the animated Christmas commercial when
Santa meets the M&M people,
While standing in front of the decorated Christmas tree,
They see each other for the very first time.
What they imagined to be unbelievable,
Suddenly became a believable reality.
They exclaimed, "He does exist!"
Santa exclaimed, "They do exist!"

The revelation was too overwhelming they each fainted,
In addition, fell on the floor.

While very creative and entertaining,
Employing the images of time-tested characters
Captures one facet of the holiday season.
However, the real message of the Christ event is purposefully absent.
The intent of the commercial was exclusively a media production,
Without displaying any explicit religious significance.

Its primary purpose was to generate financial profits for their companies.
Nevertheless, for decades
The subtle message to the children of the world,
"Fictional characters do exist!"
Many people across the globe have been taught to believe
"These characters exist".

Most rational people would be prone to say in jest
Santa Clause is real!
Rudolph the red nose reindeer is real!
The dwarfs are real!
Santa's home in the North Pole is real!
Flying reindeers are real!
The M&M people still may be questionable.

For the most part, many people know,
Because they have had a "Peek-a-boo moment",
These Christmas animations
Are only business mechanisms,
Laden with traditional folklore,
Which only brings temporary joy,
In addition to, long lasting financial obligations.

Another subtle message is,
Christmas is the season whereby we should
Expect to receive plenty of gifts,
In recognition of the birth day of Jesus Christ,
The One whom most might not personally know.
Alternatively, the name Jesus Christ,
Might have only been mentioned by them in vain.

In general,
Christmas has become the season for Christmas parties,
The time of year for receiving
Work-related bonus.
For traveling home for the holidays,
For Christmas shopping,
Sending out Christmas cards, or
Decorating a Christmas tree.
In addition, the house with wired withy Christmas lights
In addition, the receiving and exchanging of Christmas gifts.

Moreover, for some, it is the annual visit to the church,
To sing Christmas songs,
To listen to a Christmas message or
Attend special Christmas productions.

The Christ event, for many has become
More of a ritualistic activity,
However, there is a resurgence of the need to maintain
The spiritual significance and value of our sacred heritage.
The Church is commissioned
To guard the authenticity and veracity of the Biblical Record
In addition, to make certain that it is never obfuscated
By the insensitive deceptions of corporations.

The Christmas event is an iatrical historical fact,
Interwoven into the fabric of humanity.
It speaks to the people of earth,
Conveying the reality of God's love for lost humanity.
God's divine entrance through the birth of the Messiah.
Bringing the gift of
Deliverance, wholeness, and new life
To all who will believe in Jesus the Christ.

Easter is the second major encumbrance that beckons a
"Peek-a-boo, I see you", moment...
Easter is the most sacred event of the Christian church.

It represents the historic event
When Jesus Christ laid down his life
To redeem humankind, as the sacrificial Lamb of God.
Moreover, it represents the day Jesus Christ rose victoriously,
Conquering sin, death and the grave,
Assuring believers around the globe
They can trust with confidence
His completed work on the cross of Calvary.

The Cadbury commercials
Of the Chocolate Easter Bunny,
A long with Easter eggs,
In addition, with the lion who was morphed with rabbit ears,
Has no relationship whatsoever
To the resurrection of Jesus Christ from the grave.
Nor salvific benefit to the salvation of humanity.

However, we might not be able to see with our natural eyes,
Nevertheless, through the Holy Spirit,
We do clearly see into the world system.
We exclaim,

"PEEK-A-BOO, WE SEE YOU!"

We will always remember that Jesus Christ
Is the reason for the Christmas season!
God was in Jesus Christ   reconciling the world unto Himself.

We will always celebrate Easter victoriously.
It is the reality of the resurrection of our Lord and Savior Jesus Christ!
It assures us of victory, hope, and new life.
I Am the Resurrection and the life. He who believes in me will live.   John 11:25

PEEK A BOO, I SEE YOU!

ALL I WANT FOR CHRISTMAS IS...

Anatomical robots and sports video games are great fun,
However, they break or quickly become obsolete.
Shirts, socks, gloves, sweaters, and hats
Are necessary winter clothing garments
But sometimes they come to big or
Too small or just are …
Most likely, needing to be returned.
Requiring waiting in long exchange lines.

IPhone and IPad are great instruments of communication.
Each device has the capacity to help us
Instantly converse with people around the world.
However, technology changes rapidly.
Next year a new model will emerge
With more advanced features.
This gift might need to be exchanged for a newer model.

As great as these new technologies are,
Nevertheless, they also can inhibit our ability
To maintain personal contact.
The device in our hand replaces us.
Face to face, communication becomes secondary.
Although a necessary instrument
For keeping connected with the world around us,
It also can become a privacy invasive instrument.

A 90" smart television is a captivating and awesome gift.
It enhances watching sports events, and movies, etc.
Makes watching television more exciting and life-like.
Sometimes, the intended placement space is inadequate.
Sometimes, there is nothing of real value on to watch.
Sometimes, the money could have been better spent
To reduce other household indebtedness.
Nevertheless, this is a Great Gift!

All of these gifts have great value,
And would be greatly appreciated as a Christmas gift.
However, there is one that surpasses all others.
That gift I would cherish most of all.

All I would like to have for Christmas is…
The same love we had for each other
When we first met.
The same love we had for each other
When we exchanged our wedding vows.
The same love we had for each other
When we looked into the eyes of our first child.
The same love we had for each other
When we committed our lives to Jesus Christ.

All I would like to have for this Christmas is…
Your love!
With that quality of love…
We can confidently instill hope in the lives of our children.
With that quality of love…
We can proudly watch our children
Grow and develop into beautiful people.
With that quality of love...
We can feel assured that one day they, too,
Will come to love the Lord
With all of their mind, heart, and soul.

With that quality of love...
They will have learned how to always
Honor and respect their family,
Care for others who are less fortunate or in need.
Fulfill their God-given potentials
For greatness in the world.

All I would like to have for Christmas is…
That our love for God becomes purer.
Our love for each other becomes deeper.
Our love for family and friends becomes longer.
Our love for the world becomes much better.
This is all I would like to have for Christmas.

THE MAGNIFICENCE OF A MOTHERS LOVE

The Wedding Jitters

Not every daughter in the world
Has been afforded the blessing
Of being embraced by a caring,
Loving and insightful mother.
A mother who is able to bring calmness,
Quietude and wise counsel
Into an anxiety-filled experience,
Such as preparing
For that one special moment in time-
The Wedding Day!
That day, for many women,
That childhood dream has come true.

That special and very sacred day
When she and her beloved,
Standing in the presence of Almighty God,
Believing His grace providentially guided them
Into the sacred and
Mystical union of oneness.
Nervously, but lovingly stand,
Exchanging their specially prepared covenant vows.

Wedding preparations are nerve-shattering experiences.
It has the capacity to thrust one into self-doubt,
Anxiety, fear and unexpected anger
With wedding planners and bridal participants.
Having a loving and insightful mother
And understanding friends
Each step of the way, is a blessing from God!
For the bride to be,
The wedding jitters will always have to flee.
When like a child,
She can confidently lay her head
Into the comforting arms of her mother,
Hear her soothing voice softly saying,
You will always be my baby girl!
You will always be my beautiful phenomenal daughter!
I am so happy and proud of you!
God has smiled upon you!
Everything is going to be all right!

The wedding jitters will flee when she
Feels her mother's soft hand wiping her brow,
And tenderly
Drying each tear on her cheek.

Knowing that her mother's prayers
Will alway follow her
Throughout each day of her marriage,
These magnificent affections from her mother's love
Will occur to be,
The greatest gift,
Any daughter could receive.
No power can withstand
The magnificence of a mother's love calming wedding jitters.

HOW DID MAMA KNOW?

How did mama know
life would become so hard to endure?
How did mama know that sometimes I would feel like giving up
and throwing in the white towel of surrender?
How did mama know, what pain, I would have to bear,
when my husband left me, and our six children,
chasing after some young girl,
so he could get his "groove" back on.

How did mama know what to say to me,
when my foot almost slipped, and I was ready to hurt somebody,
after I learned that some strange man raped my 13-year-old baby girl,
and now she has become pregnant with that pervert's baby.
Moreover, when one of my sons, was caught-up in gang-related activity,
was caught, charged, and incarcerated in some far away prison.
How did mama know what words of wise counsel to give me
that stopped me from going on a wild rampage,
seeking revenge and justice?
Mama only had received a sixth-grade education.

How did she know what to say?
Moreover, what constructive action steps to take?

How did mama know,
When after being laid-off from my job,
I would still be able to survive.
I would still be able to
feed, clothe, and provide safe shelter for my children.
How did mama know how to help me manage my finances?
In addition, not to panic each time the bills came due?
Why did she always tell me," the Lord will make a way somehow?"

How did mama know, that when death
made an unwelcome intrusion into our family,
and snatched away the life of another one of my precious sons,
a child whom, we no longer would be able to share
the blessed presence of his life.
How did mama know what prayer to pray?
What songs to sing?
What words comforting words to say
that comforted our broken hearts,
calmed our sorrow filled spirits,
and stopped the constant flow of our tears?

How did mama know,
in the times of family crisis,
the way to turn our pain and grief
into blessed peace and hope?

How did mama know,
when she, was diagnosed with pancreatic cancer,
and doctors gave her only a few months to live. Mama knew in her spirit
that the doctors did not have the final "say so".
The longevity of her life would be determined only by God.

It was by God's grace,
that mama's life had been extended
six months longer than anyone expected
In accord with God's perfect timing,
mama transitioned into His glorious presence, and to eternal life.
Sometimes I can hear mama's sweet voice
quoting one of her favorite mantras
or singing her favorite song.
"*God is able to do immeasurably more
than all we ask or imagine,
according to his power that is at work within us!*"

*The Lord will make a way somehow
when beneath the cross I bow*

*He will take away each sorrow;
let Him have your burdens now*

*When the load bears down so heavy
the weight is shown upon my brow*

*There's a sweet relief in knowing
the Lord will make a way somehow.*

How did mama know?
Well, one day I finally sat down and asked her.
"How did you come to know so much about
the life-altering realities of living?"
Sometimes we know very little about our parents or grandparents,
or their life experiences, and struggles.
so often, we failed to take time to talk with them
or listen with care, as they attempted to share their story.
However, it is through the testimonies of our elders
that we can gain great insight,

as we struggled overcome our own personal vicissitudes.
Sometimes we do not appreciate
the struggles they had to endured,
the sacrifices they had to make in order
to ensure that we, their children,
would live in a safe space,
be able to take full advantage of the opportunities
to become successful, spiritually rooted, and grounded.
A place where we would be encouraged to excel,
to set and reach higher attainable goals
and to fulfill our God-assigned destinies.

Mama said to me, life for her, "ain't been easy".
Her journey had not been a lovely walk through
the beautiful fields, allayed with colorful purple flowers,
and sweet fragrances.
Mama said, many times, she had experienced
what it felt like to be abandoned,
confused, and lost and without hope.

Many nights, she felt the piercing stings of grief,
when death suddenly, and unexpectedly appeared,
and carried away her mother, and father,
and each of her siblings, to their final resting place.
She had experienced the unending heartaches of loneliness
She had experienced the ravages of segregation, racism, and sexism.
She had experienced the whiplashes of envy, jealousy, pride, and hatred.
She had experienced the rejection cast upon her
by family members, friends, and co-workers.

Mama said, in essence, life for her "ain't been no carefree walk down
the luxurious paths of prosperity and pleasure.
But a daily, unsettling walk down the dark, dangerous,
and winding alleyways in "the ghetto".

Mama said, sometimes she almost became homeless.
Sometimes, she had borrowed money,
just to get enough to provide food,
and shelter for us children.
Sometimes, the only job she could get
was cleaning another person's house.
Making the beds in a 2-star motel
or flipping burgers at a local fast food diner.
Sometimes, she almost had to do
anything to take care of me, and my five siblings.

Mama said again, "Child, life for me ain't been easy,
it's been very hard.
Child, there were so many times
when I just didn't know what to do.
I didn't know who to tell.
I didn't know where to go
or which way to turn.

I almost gave up, and attempted to kill myself.
But every time, my thoughts about each of my children
always stopped me from committing that tragic mistake".
Mama's eyes began to tear up as she continued to talk about the day
when my daddy walked out on us
and she was left alone,
without adequate financial resources.
That day was the most painful day in her life!
That day she attempted to end her own life
That was a troublesome day.
However, the very next day, after she regained her senses.
She made a vow to God, to live a holy life before Him and her children.
She made a commitment, to do all within her physical strength and ability,
to teach each of her children, not only how to succeed in this life,
but, most importantly, how to die

with faith in God, and hope through Jesus Christ.
Mama said, she learned how to manage
the few food stamps she received each month.
She always had enough to take care of each of us.
Mama had become a self-made culinary artist.
She learned how to draw the essence out of powdered potatoes,
powdered milk, canned spam and canned chicken.
She knew how to make welfare food taste good!
She even knew how to prepare
freshly fried fish bones, as a meat substitute.
She made the best chicken gizzards and livers,
served over rice, hot gravy and onions.
Mama did unimaginable things with black eye peas,
beans, and collard greens, simmering in ham hocks.
Mama baked the tallest and softest cornbread
we had ever seen or eaten
Somehow, she managed to find time
bake a peach cobbler pie for dessert.
Who could ever forget Mama's cooking?
She even knew how to how to doctor up
varied flavors of Kool-Aid and make it taste good.
Mama always knew how to make nutritious delicious meals for our family.

How did mama know, for the most part,
how keep us safe while growing up in the center city,
once called the ghetto?
How did mama know when we were always lying
or doing things we shouldn't be doing?
We always thought that Mama
also had eyes in the back of her head.
Nothing ever easily got past her view.

Whenever we complained about
what we did not have, or where we had to live.

Mama said, It is only by the grace of God
We are safe where we are living.
No matter what we have, be grateful.
God provided it!
No matter what it may look like,
we are truly blessed!"

How did mama come to know so much about the essentials of life?
I learned so much by listening to her,
as she shared her life stories.
I learned, basically, there were two primary sources
that provided her with constant wisdom.
She daily talked with God, about her personal struggles, trials, and real
afflictions. It was through Jesus Christ, she gained the understanding,
and the will to prevail.
She had discovered that persistent prayer,
and daily meditating on the Holy Scriptures,
renewed her strength, freed her mind,
and blessed her with insight.
The unending spiritual songs, and gospel hymns,
she would often sing or hum throughout the day,
maintained high levels of praise in her heart.

I can recall, every Sunday she walked with us
singing all of the ways back and forth to the church.
We all felt that mama intentionally kept us in church all day long
as if to keep us safe from unseen attacks from the enemy of our soul!

Long ago, mama found the help she needed in Christ.
She gained a greater appreciation for the church, by reading and meditating
on the Word of God.
She learned that the principles recorded in the Bible,
which, throughout the ages were tried, tested, were actually true.

She saw how God never failed to provide wise counsel
to everyone who trusted Him.
Therefore, mama earnestly believed in her heart, mind, and soul that the things
God did for others
He was able to do for her as well.
It was after going through her own crucibles of life
she was able to understand that
the priorities, principles, and promises of God
were all necessary things, not only
for beneficial and instructive for herself ,
but for her children as well.

How did mama live and die?
Mama was a woman of faith!
Mama was a Prayer Warrior!
Mama was a loving mother!
Mama was a wise counselor!
Mama was a phenomenal woman!
Mama was a blessed woman!
Mama was a victorious child of God!
Mama was my Mama!
Now I know how Mama Knew!

I CAN STILL HEAR MAMA SAY

In times like these you need a Savior,
In times like these you need an anchor,
Be very sure, be very sure,
Your anchor holds,
And grips the Solid Rock.
This Rock is Jesus, Yes, He's the One;
This Rock is Jesus, the only One!
Be very sure, be very sure,
Your anchor holds and grips the Solid Rock!

There is no doubt you might be living,
In difficult moments of crisis.
Each day may seem harder to go through than yesterday.
Sometimes you may begin to wonder,
If the storms will ever cease,
If the sun will ever shine again,
If the mountain of problems
Will always remain so hard to climb,
If the valley of disappointment,
Will ever pass your home,
And leave you alone?
If your midnight tears will always continue,

Or will God ever wipe your tears away?
You may also still be wondering,
Is it worth the effort to keep hope alive?

My children,
Be encouraged, and know without a doubt,
God has always been there
Keeping watch over you.
God has always been there.
Holding you in the palm of His mighty hand,
To see you through each and every trial.

God has always been there with you,
Opening unseen closed doors for you,
Which no man can ever close.

God has always been there with you,
Whenever you were about ready to throw in the towel,
Anointing your mind, heart, and soul,
With the healing balm of mercy and love.

God has always been with you,
Even when you walked away from Him,
Traveling down the dark streets of self-destruction.
His eye was not only on the little sparrow,
God was also keeping watch above you.
God has always been with you.
In the midst of your most troubling days,
And darkest nights.
Therefore, be encouraged and never give up hope.
I have discovered,
Unspeakable joy often comes,
The next morning.
Nevertheless, you have the responsibility,

To take the first step.
Make sure, your anchor holds and grips,
The Solid Rock ~ Jesus Christ!

You cannot pretend to know The Lord.
You must know, that you know, that you know,
God is real!
Jesus Christ is your only Savior.
The Holy Spirit is the source of your joy.
The strength of your life.
You will know without a doubt,
Your anchor is holding.
You have a strong grip,
When you earnestly seek to daily,
Walk and talk with God,
Read, study, and trust in His Word.
Pray with confidence knowing,
God always hears and cares about you.
God will always see you through.
There is nothing impossible for God to do.
*"Many are the afflictions of the righteous,
but the Lord delivers us from them all".*
Psalms 34:19

I pray you will discover for yourself, as I did,
God is real!
The Bible is true!
Hope is alive!
When you have embraced these realities,
Do not forget to remember,
It is your God-given assignment.
Teach these truths to your children and grandchildren,
They will also need God in their lives.
The troubling days of their generation,

May become more life-altering than ours.
If they lose hope…
Then what will they do?
To whom will they go?
No one can live without hope.
No one can live alone in the world without God.
Please give attention to the final words I have to say.
No matter what,
Always seek to walk honorably,
And respectfully, before your children.
They are always watching you.
Do not be afraid to correct them in love,
When they do wrong.
Never intentionally seek to harm them,
Physically or emotionally.
No matter if they go astray,
Always love them.
God knows how to bring them back
To the right path.
When they return and mature,
They will love, honor, and respect you,
For preparing them for their own life's journey.
Moreover, be sure, be very sure,
You take the time to lead
Your children and grandchildren,
By your spiritual example to,
The One, and Only Solid Rock, Jesus Christ!

MY AMAZING DAUGHTER

Children are a gift from the Lord; they are a reward from him.
                                            Psalm 127:3

Because God lovingly created you to be
Who you are.
I have been given an unimaginable precious gift.
A gift to treasure and love all of the days of my life.
I was afforded the privilege to love and raise
An Amazing Daughter
The moment I held her in my arms,
I knew she was special.
She opened her slanted eyes,
Looked straight at me,
Did not cry.
I think she was trying to smile!

When she was a little girl,
I knew that God had blessed me with
A Remarkable Daughter
She loved to be in the presence of people
Whom she trusted and respected.
She had a sweet, calming voice to sing
My prayers were always answered,
When she accompanied my preaching with a song.
I know God has smiled upon me with favor.
God has blessed me watch my daughter
Grow and develop in her intimate walk with the Lord
As she moved some of the unsettling changes in her life.
She has become,
A phenomenal daughter
In addition, an exceptional mother
And Grandmother, and most important,
A woman of faith
The quality of her faith
Has been an inspiration to countless people.
The depth of her spiritual insight
Has been enlightening
To young believers in Christ.
Unquestionably, she has the anointing of
The Holy Spirit upon her life.
Moreover, her love for God is effervescently
Manifested in through the nurturing
Love for her children.
The powerful preaching of the gospel,
The elegant praises
Displayed in her liturgical dances.

In addition, the love and compassion
She has for all people.
I have been truly blessed by, God,

Because of my special daughter.
She was exquisitely created,
By the loving hand of Almighty God.
Because of my daughter,
I am an exceedingly blessed man.
My life has a clearer purpose.
I know the real sources of my joy and strength.
I know I am deeply loved.
Because of my daughter,
I hope that I have become a better man.
A better father.
A father, whom she will always be proud to say
That's my dad!

ALL BECAUSE OF MY DAUGHTER

Children are a gift from the Lord; they are a reward from him. Psalm 127:3

I have received a precious treasure from the Lord!
I have another **amazing** daughter
She challenges me when I am wrong
In addition, she encourages me
When she knows I am right.

I have a **remarkable** daughter
She provides wise counsel
When I feel discouraged
And laughter, and joy when I am angry

I have a **phenomenal** daughter
She provides the best medical advice when I am sick
And financial resources when I am in need
I have a **Godly** daughter
Who loves Jesus Christ

Moreover, that same love
Which was deeply embedded in her heart
She lovingly extends to me.

Because of my daughter's love
I am an exceedingly blessed man
My life has a clearer purpose
I know the real value of my family
I know I am deeply respected and appreciated

Because of my daughter
I hope that I have become a better man
A better father
A father, whom she will always be proud to say
That's my dad!

WHO NEEDS FRIENDS LIKE THESE?

Close friends are very special people.
They enjoy doing crazy things together with you.
They always tease each other,
They always fuss with each other,
They always complain to each other,
Sometimes, they become angry at each other.
However, they always stick close to each other,
Through the good times or the difficult times.
Sometimes they remain friends to the very end of life.
Who needs friends like these?
Close friends know how to help others enjoy life.
They are not afraid to flow
With the changing times,
Yet maintain a wholesome balance
In their relationships,
Between enjoyment and insanity.
Into every personal relationship

They bring:
Creative things,
Exciting things,
Colorful things,
Out of the box things.
They bring laughter,
They bring singing,
They bring good eating,

They bring healthy exercising,
They bring hope,
They bring blessings,
They bring life.
Who needs friends like these?

Those same close friends know how to love you!
They have an intimate love relationship with God,
They reflect His radiance every time
They are with you.
They pray for your well-being.
They assist you with unexpected financial blessing,
They encourage you when you feel discouraged.

They stand by your side during crises,
They call, "to see how you are doing".
They celebrate with you
On your special days.
They travel for miles to visit you,
Just because…
Who needs friends like these?
I know I do!

ALL BECAUSE OF A TREE!

Daddy, why is there so much violence,
And trouble around the world?
Why do people say and do
So many mean and evil things to each other?
Will they hate us too?
Will they try to harm us too?
When I grow up
Will I become like them too?
Daddy, can you tell me,
Why they became so angry with The Creator?
Well, my son let me tell you!
All of the world's troubles began
Because of one disobedient act
Against a beautiful and, special tree in a garden,
The Creator commanded them
Never to touch… but they did!
Since that day,
All manner of evil infested the planet.
However, there are two other glorious trees,
Designed by the Creator,
Which provided healing, and restoration,
To all believers around the world,
Who embraced His provisions of grace and mercy.

Understand, everything continues to happen,
Because of a tree!

THE TREE OF JUDGEMENT IN THE GARDEN OF EDEN
By the brook, I stood in my entire splendor
In a garden, only the creator's hands could have made
The embodiment of my being, irresistible, in the sunlight or the shade
The seductiveness of my beauty
Not yet seen by any woman or any man
My justification I was not even sure of
It was all in God's plan for me to understand
He gave mankind a choice after creating them
"Don't touch don't taste the fruit of me"!
Lustful eyes taught their hearts disobedience
Casting the world into sin through their seed
All because of a tree!

THE TREE OF REDEMPTION AT CALVARY
If you ever came to the meadow there, I was
Strong, rooted and deep in the earth
Really never was I alone, flocks arrived frequently
To give the master praise as they perched
Suddenly a shaking off the dirt, I was being uprooted from the ground
Leaves shaking, boughs were breaking
I was making an awful sound
It was not through old age or disease
That I was beginning to die
But being cut down from the roots
Why? I didn't understand, and why just now?
I was created for just this season
For the Master to be stretched up high
I endured the nails, I felt his blood,
He gave His life, redeemed humankind, for this, He had to die.
All because of a tree!

THE TREE OF LIFE IN HEAVEN

I am the bearer of my own essence, called life
A new beginning for eternity, the ending of all strife
I have obtained a place in Heaven for the healing of the land
Moreover, all who sup with the Master will taste of the fruit it has

You have been obedient to His laws and statues
In all you've said and done
Come on up good and faithful servants
Welcome home, well done, all my daughters and all my sons
All because of a tree!

IF TREES COULD TALK

Grandma, why are those people so mean to us?
What did we do to them that caused them to hate us so much?

They are always stepping on us.
Always carving on us.
Always killing us, and then cut us into pieces.
Always dragging us away from our homeland
To some strange land.

Sometimes they set fire around us, and burn us to the ground.
Grandma, what did we do to cause them to hate us so much?
Will they kill us too?

Gather around me, my beloved children.
Let me answer you, and try to encourage your hearts.
It is true, some of those creatures had devastated our environment.
They stranded our forest inhabitants, severed our family relationships
By cutting them down.

They did drag them out of our rainforests,
Which they were specially designated by God to protect.

It is true, they were cut into pieces
And then shipped to some strange land,
Never to be seen or heard from again.
However, my children do not despair!

There were some of those same creatures
Who really do value our presence, and contributions.
They came to understand that we too were specifically designed by Almighty God,
And endowed with an awesome capacity to oxygenate the entire planet.
We each had been strategically placed around the world
To restrain the ravaging storm waters,
To provide shelter for a myriad of forest residents,
And to protect the earth from major catastrophes.

We also were wonderful, and beautifully designed by Almighty God
To withstand each of the changing seasons of time.
So, do not despair, my children, there is still hope!
Needless to say, we must remain grateful for those creatures
Who made great sacrifices to protect us.
This is one of the reasons why we are still here!

Nevertheless, as you can see
I've been here a very long, long, long time.
My children, now take a closer look at my scars.
There is a story behind each one of them,
Although they may be faded by time,
If you look a little closer,
You will see, they are still visible.

I was not born nor nurtured with these scars.
Like you, my skin was smooth and almost perfect.

Each year I was growing taller, and bursting with vitality.
Every day I was greeted with the fresh mist of the morning dew.
My limbs were growing stronger, and stronger.
On every limb, beautiful green leaves were appearing everywhere!
I could feel the sparkling, warm embrace of the rising sun
As it imparted rays of energy from my crown to the deep fibers of my roots.
Early each morning a host of different birds settled on my limbs
Singing beautiful melodies of praise.

Children, know this for sure,
My life has not always been easy, as each of these scars will verify.
I have been through many severe lightning storms.
I have been through hurricanes, tornadoes, blizzards, and earthquakes.
But I'm still here!

However, there came a day when I thought my life was at its end.
What had happened to my parents, relatives
And so many of my friends were about to happen to me.
I was so afraid!

Grandma, tell us what happened?
Were you really that scared
That you thought you were going to die?
Yes, I was! Let me tell you.
One day, two strange creatures
Came hiking into our quiet community.
I had never seen that kind of creature in all of my days.
They were not scary to look at, but beautiful creatures.
I had no idea where they might have come from.
They even uttered strange sounds which I nor others
Had ever heard before.

Although they were beautiful creatures
They had little regard for our home environment

Or our young baby trees.
As they were tramping through our homeland
They were carelessly crushing our baby trees into the ground.
All we could do was sigh, groan, and shed our leaves in protest.
It mattered not. They could not hear or interpret our cries.
From that moment up until today,
Our beloved community, our family our lives,
Have never been the same.

The next day those same two creatures came back!
This time one of the creature took a very sharp object
And embedded it deep into my side
While carving an unusual image,
With strange symbols on the inside.
When the other creature read it
They quickly ran away chasing after each other.

Can you see that scar?
It's still here, right over there!
Grandma, did you cry?
Grandma, does it still hurt?
No child! Sometimes, only the memory still hurts.
The most frightening time came. years later.
Many more strange creatures came
With very big and loud sounding things.
Soon thereafter, I saw my parents, my brothers, and sisters,
Then other family members and friends,
Suddenly fall to the ground.
It sounded like loud claps of thunder all day long.
I watched in horror as each family member was cut into pieces
And then slowly dragged away, far from our motherland.
These scars are very deeply embedded within.
You may feel my pain, locked up inside of me because of our symbiotic union.
What I had felt you can now feel.

Grandma, is there any hope for us?
Will we be scared for life too?
Will we too be cut down into pieces,
And dragged away from our homeland?
No, my children, not now.
Because there are many more of those beautiful creatures
Who have come to appreciate our presence,
And the vital contributions we are creating for the entire planet.
Moreover, they love us too.

One day you will grow very old too,
And tell your own stories
To your children and grandchildren.

LIFE IS LIKE A VAPOR

When the shades of light begin to be lowered
And the light dimly squeezes through the veiled corners.
When the white ivory becomes tarnished,
And invisible foes beneath the surface
Send their muffled unwanted drum beat to the extractor.
When the black strands change color
And hide never to appear again.
When the twin oaks and the extended branches
Become weak and weather-beaten.
When a new Pharaoh arises,
And the Beloved Community
No longer remembers your name or your contributions.
When the sands of time had released its last granular,
And life evaporates like a vapor.
It appeared for a moment in time, and then,
It is gone.
The vapor appeared, now it is forever gone!
Do we live only to wonder,
When will our life evaporate as a vapor?

IF I WAS CREATED AS AN EYE

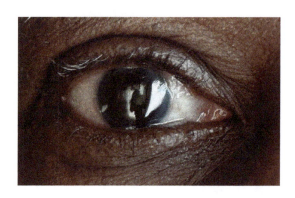

How amazing it would be
If I was created just as an eye!
I wonder if
My ocular vision would be greater than the eagles?
I wonder if
I would be able to scan the depths of space
Exceeding the capacity of a Hubble space telescope?
I wonder if
I would be able to probe into people's lives
To see what has been veiled to a natural man?

If I were just an eye
How amazing that would be?
I could see myself
As the most influential person in the world.

I could see myself
Surround by people waiting to receive
Special insights from me.

If I was created just to be an eye
I would be important!
I would be awesome!
I would be loved!
I would be amazing!

If I was created just to be an eye
I would be… I would be…
I would be…
I would be estranged from everyone.
I would have no friends.
I would be all alone.
I would be frightened.
I would be of little value to everyone.

Primarily because,
I would have no ears to hear them
I would have no tongue to speak to them
I would have no hands to touch them
I would have no feet to walk with them
I would have no mind to think with them
I would have no heart to feel anything with them

I would be all alone
Asking God why did you create me like this?
It would be pure misery and hopelessness.

To be created just as an eye
Was never God's design or plan for humanity.
Almighty God in His infinite wisdom
Created mankind in His own image to be whole and holy.
Mankind was created as the majestic apex of all creation.
Upon completion God declared
Everything to be very good!
Every part of our being
Body, spirit, and soul
Is synchronistic, and vital to our well-being,
And spiritual functionality.
Harmoniously working toward the advancement
Of the Kingdom of God
Through faith in Jesus Christ.

Moreover, the Holy Scripture declares:
The way God designed our bodies
is a model for understanding our lives together as a church:
every part dependent on every other part,
the parts we mention and the parts we don't,
the parts we see and the parts we don't.
one part hurts, every other part is involved in the hurt,
and in the healing.
If one part flourishes,
every other part enters into the exuberance.

I Corinthians 12:26

THE GIFTS OF GOD

Unconditional **Love** lifted us up to Amazing Grace
Grace led us to Saving Faith
Faith led us to Majestic Peace
Peace led us to Unspeakable Joy
Joy led us to Blessed **Hope**
Love, Grace, Faith, Peace, Joy, and Hope   Presented us to Jesus Christ
Jesus Christ gave us the Crown of **Victory**

WE CRY ABBA, FATHER

*The Spirit you received does not make you slaves
so that you live in fear again;
rather, the Spirit you received brought about your adoption to sonship,
and by him we cry, "Abba, Father."*   Romans 8:15

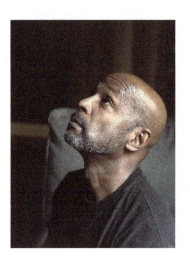

Abba, Father, hallowed be Your Holy name,
There is no one like my, "Abba, Father" in all of the creation.
You are God, alone!

We praise and magnify Your Holy Name.
Humbly, we pray that our lives,
Will be an expression of
Your, love, grace, and mercy.

Thank you for the indwelling presence of the Holy Spirit,
Blessing us with the honor of adopting us
As your new children in Christ.
You are our heavenly Abba, Father.
Abba, Father, our entire being is exceedingly grateful,
If we had the capacity to speak in thousands of languages,
They would all be inadequate to express our soul's gratitude.

Abba, Father, thank you for loving us so much,
Sending us your one and only Son, Jesus,
Who willingly laid down His life,
To save messed up people like us.
Abba, Father, how you came into the world,
Seeking only to save, lost, and broken sinners,
Who were just like, we used to be.
Your love…
It is incomprehensible,
It is inexplicable,
It is unfathomable,
It is awesome,
It is amazing!
We are so grateful that, You came into the world!

Abba, Father, we believe that we are redeemed.
We are set free by amazing grace.
We are no longer afraid to live,
Moreover, to walk by faith.
The shackles, and strongholds in our lives,
Have been broken,
As a result of the blood of Jesus Christ,
Moreover, the power of the Holy Spirit,
Completely eradicated the power and vestiges of sin.
Heavenly, Abba, Father, thank you for daily
Cleansing and empowering us to live holy.
Moreover, thank you for Your eternal promise,
I am He who blots out your transgressions.
For My own sake and remembers your sins no more.
Isaiah 43:25

Abba, Father, thank you for loving us so much!
Abba, Father, thank you for anointing us with your peace,
A peace that surpasses all human understanding.

Abba, Father, thank you for filling our soul with your joy,
A joy that is exceedingly great,
The world can never take it away.

Abba, Father, thank you for enveloping us with hope.
A hope that is eternally blessed,
A hope that soon, will become realized.
A glorious hope, in which, one day,
We will all behold the face of
Our Lord and Savior, Jesus Christ.
Moreover, humbly kneel before
Your throne in glory…
Like the heavenly host,
Jubilantly proclaim forever,

Thou art worthy, Abba, Father,
to receive glory, and honor, and power;
for Thou hast created all things:
and for Thy pleasure, they are and were created. Revelation 4:11
Abba, Father, today, we totally recommit ourselves
To do your sacred will.
In Jesus' name, Amen.

MISSION IMPOSSIBLE

Cure the sick, bring the dead back to life
Cleanse those with skin diseases,
Force demons out of people   Matthew 10:8
With man, this is impossible, but with God, all things are possible   Mark 10:27

Lord Jesus, did I hear you correctly?
You expect me to do each of these commands on your behalf
I do not have the power to complete just one of those commands
I am only human
I am not a medical doctor
I am not a miracle worker
I do not have a dermatological degree
I am not an exorcist
I am just an ordinary human being
Those expectations sound to me like
A mission impossible

I almost forgot
You will never expect me to do anything on your behalf
Without first enabling me
Through the anointing of the Holy Spirit
Without undergirding me with the Word of God
Therefore, I believe, I can accomplish this mission
Greater is He who is in me
Than any demon in the world, including Satan
You have not given to me a spirit of weakness or fear
But of power, love and a clear mind

Lord Jesus, I believe
You are the Son of the living God
You came to Earth
To heal and save our world of lost sinners

Who were just like me
Lord, I am available to do your will
I believe, I can do all things through
Your powerful name
And by the Holy Ghost's anointing
Your mission is not an impossible mission
May God's will be done!

THE SHAKING OF FOUNDATIONS

If the foundations are destroyed, what can the righteous do? Psalm 11:3

Although the cause of evil ostentatiously seems to prevail
Although the foundational ethical and moral principles
That make us a civilized people ~
Justice, love, integrity, freedom, and truth,
Appear to be disintegrating before our eyes

Although these divine principles, which are ordained by Almighty God,
Yet treated with disdain, and summarily abandoned by many,
Yet the Word of God always prevails

These fundamental principles are indomitable, irrefragable and eternal
They can never become null or void by the
Unprincipled, nefarious or pernicious acts
Or pronouncements of humankind

Nevertheless, throughout the millennia of time
The consequential acts of defiance by humankind
Always results in the shaking of foundational structures

These ethical and moral foundational principles
And its corresponding institutions, though shaken
Nevertheless, they have never been completely destroyed by humankind

The institution of the family
The institution of marriage
The institution of justice
The institution of education
The institution of faith

These violent shakings today
Are a result of the abandonment of the Word of God
And humanities embracing of the unholy alliance of
Deceit, lies, and injustice
Although the cause of evil seems to prosper
Although the structures of our world are being violently shaken
God is still in His Holy Sacred Realm
Keeping watch upon His own

If the foundations are shaken, what can the righteous do?
In the midst of the shaking
God encourages and enables the righteous to
Keep on praying
Keep on giving
Keep on serving
Keep on believing
Keep on forgiving
Keep on teaching
Keep on trusting in God
Keep on keeping on
With the understanding ~ God is always in control
Whatever circumstances, conditions or challenges
Humankind or Satan had meant for evil purposes
God through, Jesus the Christ, has already reversed them all
To work for our wellbeing and to His glory

We know that in all things God works for the good
Of those who love him,
Who have been called according to his purpose.
Romans 8:28

EAGLES DO FALL

*They that wait upon the LORD shall renew their strength;
they shall mount up with wings as eagles.*   Isaiah 40:31

God created eagles with powerful wings to fly high above mountaintops,
and to soar through the beautiful sky with elegant ease.
God endowed the eagle with extraordinary sensor cells
specially designed for long distance focus and clarity of vision,
enabling them to spot small objects miles away.
God created the eagle with powerful talons
to grasp prey sometimes larger
and a little heavier than itself.
God clothed the eagle from its large head to its wing-tail
with an array of seven thousand
magnificent layers of colorful, weather resistant feathers.
God created the eagle with a broad breast,
protecting its heart and other vital organs
with a strong rib cage enclosure.
God blessed the eagle with the maternal instincts it needed
to determine when it was time
to release its eaglets from the nest,
so they too could learn how to fly high
above the mountaintops,
and soar elegantly through the beautiful blue skies.

Pride leads to destruction, and arrogance to downfall

It is a rare occurrence, but majestic eagles do fall from the sky,
down to the ground, and could die.
There usually are three primary reasons
why these magnificent eagles fall,
either it was defeated in a fight with a stronger eagle.

It had starved due to lack of sufficient food
or a hunter senselessly shot it down.

God created the eagle to fly high above the mountaintops,
and to soar elegantly through the beautiful blue skies
Moreover, God created humankind
as the apex of His creation.
Moreover, God declared it, "very good".
God crowned them with honor and glory,
surpassing all other created things.

There was nothing in the entire order of creation
that was deemed greater than humanity
because God created them in His image.

Like unto the magnificent eagles,
humankind is endowed with the capacity
to ascend into the heavens, and soar high above
the mountains of its life-threatening experiences.

The mountains of disbelief, disappointment, and discouragement
the mountains of depression, despair and death
Like unto the majestic eagles whose destiny was threatened
by the aggression of others, inadequate nutritional sustenance,
and an unseen predator, humanity likewise,
had to be aware of the injurious physical and spiritual health conditions,
and of the unseen nemesis
which could cast them out of the sky
down to the ground, and left to die.

God, whose heart full of compassion and immeasurable love
informed mankind of those dangerous predators
that had the capacity to deceive them, exalt them,
give them temporary power, and then suddenly,
cast them out of their self- exalted positions
down to the ground, leaving them to die.

Pride and arrogance toward their Creator
always lead to disobedience and defiance.
These would be the infectious causal factors
that would lead to the fall from the sky
just like a sick or wounded eagle.

Pride and arrogance caused Lucifer to fall from his exalted position in Heaven
to be eternally condemned in hell
Pride and arrogance caused Adam and Eve
to be cast out of the Garden of Eden,
and to meander all the days of their life
in the wilderness of tears because of their disobedience

Pride and arrogance caused King Saul to lose his throne,
and fall into the chambers of mental illness
Pride and arrogance caused the mighty Samson,
King David and his son Solomon
to fall from divine favor, and strength,
into beds of weakness and infamy

Pride and arrogance cause the great Pharaohs of Egypt, the emperors of Rome
the Presidents of major nations, Dictators of third-world countries,
religious leaders, politicians, professional athletes, school teachers,
musicians, lawyers, parents,
Creator and our God has declared
that all of humanity has fallen
due to our acts of disobedience and defiance
We all had been attacked, wounded and infected in our souls
by the cancerous venom of pride and arrogances
We all had become an offense to our Creator and God
Everyone is subject to being thrust out of the sky,
cast down to the ground, and left to die.
Unseen to the eyes of some, many majestic eagles
had been rescued by the mercy of others, and restored to wholeness,
God in His infinite wisdom, before laying the infrastructure
of the universe and the earth,
knowing the vulnerability of our humanity,
made provisions for our restoration and eternal safety
The Ancient of Days took upon himself the nature of our humanity,
but without the weakness to fall or cast down by any predator

The Ancient of Days
willingly sacrificing His own life, shed His own blood, died upon a cross
On the third days raised Himself from the grave
with all authority and power
to restore the fracture between humanity
and their Creator, Almighty God.

Everyone who submits himself to his healing balm,
and loving care, will be forgiven of their sin,
cleansed, and restored.
They will be enabled to soar once again,
with new wisdom, confidence, power, and determination.
They will be enabled to soar again with agape love
for their Creator and God.
They will be enabled to soar again trusting God
with all of their mind, heart, and soul.
They will be enabled to soar again with the spiritual vision of an eagle.
They will be enabled to soar again with new strength to hold onto the truth.
They will be enabled to soar again with an anointing
that can withstand any storm.
They will be enabled to soar again with the breastplate of righteousness.
They will be enabled to soar again with the crown of victory
declaring how they were able to over their predators.
They will be enabled to soar again with elegance,
flying into to their blessed destiny.
but to continue flying high above the mountains.
Look at them, they are flying high and soaring on wings like an eagle!
God is smiling! In addition, God said, "Very Good"!

LORD, I DON'T WANT TO GO THERE

Lord, I don't want to go there,
But my mind is pressing me so hard, I can't control it.
My mind is pressing me to go to a place
Where there is deep, deep, deep darkness.
A place where tears unceasingly flow.
A dwelling place for depression.
A dwelling place for uncontrollable anger.
A dwelling place for stress and fear.
A dwelling place for excruciating pain.
A dwelling place for unending loneliness.

Lord, my mind is trying to take me to a place,
Where I don't want to go.
The dwelling place of hopelessness.
The dwelling place of pure evil.
The dwelling place of despair.
The dwelling place of terror.
The dwelling place of death.
Lord, I don't want to go there.
I am weak.
I am so tired.
I can't take it any longer.
I can't control my mind.

I can't deliver myself.
I can't save myself.
I don't want to go to that place!
I don't want to go…
I don't want to…
I don't want…, I don't, I don't…
Lord, help me!
Lord, deliver me!
Lord, save me!

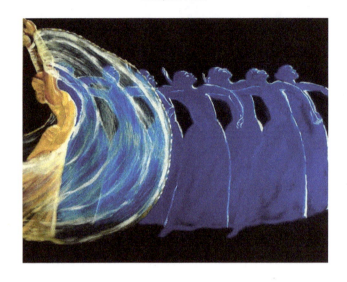

Thank you Lord, for saving me!
*In my distress I called to the Lord;
I called out to my God.
From His temple, He heard my voice;
my cry came to His ears.* 2 Samuel 22:7

DON'T GIVE UP NOW!

So, you find life to be very hard!
Well, nobody said,
"It will be easy!"
Life for me, as well, has not been easy.
It has been very hard,
Nevertheless, I never gave up!
However, I must admit,
There were days when I almost did.
Nevertheless, by the grace of God,
I did not give up!

I have seen many frightening midnight atrocities,
I have walked through many
Troubling, and dangerous waters.
I felt the agonizing strikes of injustice.
I shed many tears for my children and people.
I know what it feels like to be
Angry, lonely, and afraid for your life.
I know what it feels like to be
Poor, jobless, homeless and hungry.
I know what it feels like to
Work from sunrise to sunset
With insufficient financial benefit.

I know what it feels like to
Build a makeshift shelter for your family,
With whatever parts you can find.
Life for me has not been easy,
It has been very hard.
Nevertheless, by the grace of God,
I did not give up!

I know that you are living in a time
Many generations removed from mine.
The rapid advancement of new technologies,
Its invasive intrusion into every aspect of your life,
The changing ethnic demographics of the world,
Issuing forth, new denigrating immigration policies,
The ever-changing social norms,
Destabilizing the primary institutions of the land,

The rising discord amongst the nations of the world,
Standing at the precipice,
Pressing toward the possible annihilation of the Earth.
Although, it appears that everything has coalesced,
The cost of household living,
Health care, and continuing educational expenses,
Is rising precipitously,
Causing great concern and consternation,
For everyone.
Nevertheless, by the grace of God,
Do not give up!

Keep pressing onward!
Life does not have the final word!
Continue to run the race
That has been set before you with faith in God.

The race is not given to the swift
nor the battle to the strong,
but to those who endure until the end.
Ecclesiastes 9:11

Keep moving forward!
You have come too far to turn back now!
Press toward the mark for the prize of
the high calling of God in Christ Jesus.
Philippians 3:14

Keep on standing!
God never told us to
"Hang in there" that is a sign of defeat.
Instead, God admonishes us to "stand".
Therefore, put on the complete armor of God, so that you will be able to
[successfully] resist and stand your ground in the evil day [of danger],
and having done everything [that the crisis demands to stand firm [in your place,
fully prepared, immovable, victorious]. Ephesians 6:13

Keep persevering!
We know that suffering produces perseverance;
perseverance, character; and character, hope. And hope does not put us to shame,
because God's love has been poured out into our hearts
through the Holy Spirit, who has been given to us. Romans 5:3-5

Keep striving for excellence!
A vast host of great achievers surrounds you.
The heights of great people,
Reached and kept,
Was never achieved by sudden flight,
But, they, while their companions slept,
We were toiling, upward in the night.

Keep trusting in The Lord!
There is no failure in The Lord!
Jesus never gave up on you!
Jesus yielded his life as an atonement for our sin.
He endured the agony of the cross.
He was wounded for our transgressions,
He was bruised for our iniquities;
The chastisement for our peace was upon Him
And by His stripes, we are healed. Isaiah 53:5

On the third day, He arose,
The victor over, sin, death and the grave,
Having all power and authority in His hands

Jesus never gave up!
For the joy set before him,
he endured the cross, scorning its shame,
and sat down at the right hand of the throne of God.
Hebrews 12:2

Keep believing!
Because Jesus never gave up on us,
As believers, we can have complete victory
Over the vicissitude's of life.
Moreover, those whom he predestined
he also called, and those whom he called he also justified,
and those whom he justified he also glorified. Romans 8:30

Keep attempting to understand!
Life is hard!
Life is challenging!
Life is purposeful!
Life is enjoyable!
Life is blessed with possibilities!

As long as you continue to walk with God,
You will remain more than a conqueror,
Through Jesus Christ!
I never gave up!
So, make this your personal mantra…
By the grace of God,
I will never give up!

MY LIFE WITHOUT YOU

*Therefore, shall a man leave his father and his mother
and shall cleave unto his wife and they shall be one flesh.*

God in His infinite wisdom
Created us with certain experiences and relationships
That is essential to our well-being
And to the fulfillment of our
Purpose and eternal destination
Sometimes in our effort to resolve condition and circumstances
We in our human facility devaluate God's will
In addition, often to our determent exalt our own
Consequently, those institutions, which God ordained
To bring us stability and peace
Are substituted for temporary relief
And unimaginable grief and pain

There are somethings that were meant to remain permanently bonded
If unwittingly or intentionally separated it would be analogous to having
A sailboat without a sail…drifting in the storms without control
A flashlight without batteries…in the gross darkness with no light
An umbrella without waterproof covering…no protective covering in storms
Eyeglasses without lenses…no corrective vision
Car keys without the car…no actual means of transportation
IPhone without a Sims card…no effective communication tool
Apple pie without apples…essence is missing only a semblance of reality

The cross without Jesus…no living savior
Joy without the Holy Ghost…sheer emotionalism

God in His infinite destined
Decreed that no matter what force comes against His Word
God's word will always remain irrefragable
God decreed that some things would always remain
Intricately and eternally intertwined
God's grace and mercy will always remain permanently bonded with His love
Our testimony is like the biblical sage of antiquity
Surely, goodness and mercy
shall follow me all the days of my life
and I shall dwell in the house of the Lord forever.

Psalm 23:6

One thing I ask from the Lord, this only do I seek
That I may dwell in the house of the Lord
All the days of my life
To gaze on the beauty of the Lord
And to seek him in his temple.

Psalm 27:4

Therefore, my life without you
Would be incomplete
Misdirected, without protective covering

I would be walking in the darkness alone
I would be devoid of delight, peace, and hope
Therefore, by the grace of God
I humbly recommit myself to you
To do all that I can to keep our relationship
Holy, strong, and blessed by Almighty God.
So help me God.

SO YOU THINK IT NO LONGER MATTERS

Train up a child in the way he should go
And when he is old,
He will not depart from it.   Proverbs 22:6

Though the cause of evil prospers
Yet 'tis truth alone that's strong.
Truth forever on the scaffold
Wrong forever on the throne,
Yet that scaffold sways the future and behind the dim unknown
Standeth God within the shadows keeping watch above his own. - Longfellow
These are the new norms for the world today!
Truth no longer matters!
Lying matters more;
Everybody is a prevaricator,
From the President to the preachers.
The politicians to the parents,
The news reporters to the prognosticators,
The children to the teachers,
Everybody lies!
Justice no longer matters!
What used to be acts of violence,
Is now considered permissible;

What used to be immoral practices,
Is now considered acceptable;
What used to be a blatant crime,
Is now considered justifiable;
What used to be dishonorable,
Is now considered honorable.

These are the new norms for the world today!
God's word is antithetical!
Life is expendable!
Immigration is unacceptable!
Death is inevitable!
Climate change is unbelievable!
Educational support is unavailable!
Financial indebtedness is unavoidable!
Incarcerations are expectable!
Eldercare is nonsensical!
Health services are not negotiable!
Love lifestyles are indistinguishable!
World peace is implausible…
Some people think it no longer matters
What we believe, say, or do.
However, our children are listening,
Our children are watching,
Our children are learning,
Our children believe,
What we say, do, believe…does matter!
What the next generation will become
Is directly reflective of what we taught them.
Therefore, everyone must consider wisely
Whose words we will speak over our children.
We must understand
Life and death are in the power of the tongue
When declaring what norms matter the most

For the survival of the world.
We can either choose
The present world's vacillating ideologies and systems,
Or, on the other hand,
Trust the veracity of the Bible, which is
The Word of God.
Choose to trust the Bible which is the Word of God.
These are the unchangeable normative realities,
"It is impossible for God to lie".
Hebrews 8:16
God is not human, that he should lie,
Not a human being,
That he should change his mind.
Does he speak and then not act?
Does he promise and not fulfill? Numbers 23:19

All life matters to God,
Christ came that we might have life,
In addition, that, more abundantly.
The truth matters to God.
Satan is the father of all lies,
No liar shall ever enter the Kingdom of God.
Justice matters to God.
He has shown you, O mortal, what is good.
Moreover, what does Jehovah require of you?
To act justly and to love mercy
and to walk humbly with your God.
Micah 6:8

Love Matters to God!
How one teaches or treats our children matters to God.
It would be better for them to be thrown into the sea
with a millstone tied around their neck
than to cause one of these little ones to stumble.

Luke 17:2
If anyone says, "I love God,"
but hates his brother, he is a liar.
For anyone who does not love his brother,
Whom he has seen,
Cannot love God,
Whom he has not seen.
John 4:20

Acceptance of Jesus Christ, as Lord,
Matters to God.
God exalted him to the highest place
And gave him the name that is above every name,
That at the name of Jesus every knee should bow,
in heaven and on earth and under the earth,
And every tongue acknowledge that Jesus Christ is Lord,
To the glory of God the Father. Philippians 2:10-11
Failure to embrace the Word of God
Has eternal consequences
That should matter to all of us.
Each person is destined to die once,
And after that comes judgment,
Then I saw a great white throne and him who was seated on it.
The earth and the heavens fled from his presence,
and there was no place for them.
Moreover, I saw the dead, great and small,
standing before the throne, and books were opened.
Another book was opened, which is the book of life.
The dead were judged according to what they had done
as recorded in the books
Each person was judged according to what they had done.
Then death and Hades were thrown into the lake of fire.
The lake of fire is the second death.
Anyone whose name was not found written in the book of life

Was thrown into the lake of fire.
What one says, does and believes
Does matter at the end!
The eternal designation of our soul matters to God.
It is not too late for anyone to change their mind.
God's desire is that everyone choose life and not death.
There is a way that appears to be right to humanity,
However, that way inevitably leads to destruction and eternal death.
It really does matter!

WHO REALLY CARES?

What have I done that is so terrible?
Why do people hate me so much?
They do not know me.
They never talked with me.
What have I done that is so terrible?

Do they hate me because
I am a girl?
Do they hate me because of
The color of my skin?
Do they hate me because of
Where I was born?
Do they hate me because
I speak a different language?
Do they hate me because
I am ugly?

Do they hate me because
My family is poor?
Do they hate me because
I worship God differently?

Why do they hate me?
What have I done that is so terrible?
I am so afraid!
The world is too big and scary!
I am alone!
I do want to live too!
I am not sure…
I guess the only safe place is…
Does anyone really care?

Christ came that she might have life,
And have it more abundantly.
Do you care?

AMBER-QUOCIOUS FRIENDS

What does the word "amber-quocious" mean?
You will not find it in an ordinary dictionary.
It is a compound word:
"Amber" ~ a gentle gold light that can be seen by everyone.
"Quocious" ~ something that is continuous.

Amber-quocious friends are
Friends who stick closer than a brother or sister.
In the world today, this is a rare quality.

Friends, whom you cannot speak about,
Without speaking about the other.
It seemed as though they were,
Intentionally designed by God,
To be continual friends.

Their names are as common as
George Burns and Gracie Allen
Mickey Mouse and Minnie Mouse
Porky Pig and Bugs Bunny
Fred Flintstone and Barney Rubble

Eggs and Bacon
Coffee and Donuts
Peanut butter and Jelly
Spaghetti and Meatballs
Mary and Joseph
Paul and Silas
Priscilla and Aquila
Barack and Michelle Obama

Space and Time
Sun and Moon
Day and Night
The universe is full of amber-quocious partners
I am so glad to have you as
My very special
Amber-quocious Friends.

THE HEALING CORRIDORS OF FAITH

Within the Healing Corridors of God,
Through the sacrificial atonement of Jesus Christ,
All of our brokenness and sins shall be healed!
Through the majestic, and magnificent name of Jesus,
We shall be delivered!
We no longer will be afraid of the darkness!
We no longer will be paralyzed by fear!
We no longer will live in hopelessness!
In Jesus Christ, we will be set free,
From the power, and penalty of sin!
Just one drop of His precious blood,
Shed for us at Calvary,
Anointing the crown of our head,

Shall completely heal every aspect of our life!
Beneath the foot of the cross of Jesus Christ
We shall find healing and redemption.
All of our feelings of depression will be eradicated!
All of our feelings of sorrow, and loneliness will be eliminated!
All of our feelings of guilt, and shame will be expiated!
All of our iniquity and sins will be exterminated!
We will become a new creation in Christ!
Because of the resurrecting power of Jesus Christ,
We can walk confidently by faith
Through each of
The Healing Corridors of God.

HALLELUJAH! I CAN SEE!

The Light is so close!
The Light is shining so bright!
The Light is blinding!
I can't see! I can't see!
O God, I can't see!
I am blind! I am blind!
O my God, I am blind!
Great is thy faithfulness.
Morning by morning new mercies I see!
The Light is majestic!
The Light is Marvelous!
The Light is Glorious!
God is The Light!
Glory! Glory to God!
Glory in the highest!
Jesus is the Light of life!
I am blind, but now, I can really see!
Hallelujah! I can see!

LORD, SOMETHING IS MISSING

Something within me that holdeth the reins
Something within me that banishes pain
Something within me I cannot explain
All that I know, there is something within

Have you that something, that burning desire?
Have you that something, that never doth tire?
Oh, if you have it, that heavenly fire
Let the world know there is something within

Lord, I know that Thou art my God and there is no other
I know that I am wonderfully created in Thy Image
I know that by Thy grace
I am saved and being sanctified
Through the precious shed blood of Jesus Christ
Lord, I know that I have gone through the waters of baptism
I know that I am a member of a good church family
I know that I am actively engaged in many leadership capacities
Within my church and community
I know that no weapon formed against me shall prosper
I know that weeping may endure for the night
Nevertheless, joy comes in the morning

I know that I can do all things through Christ
Who strengthens me!

Although I am trying my best
To be a positive example of a Christian
Before my family and others
Nevertheless, in spite of all
The good that I do and try to become
Something within me is still missing

No one else can see what is missing
Nevertheless, O Lord, You can
No one else can feel my emptiness
Nevertheless, O Lord, You can
No one else can answer my earnest prayers
Nevertheless, O Lord, You can

Sometimes my faith is entangled with fear
Sometimes my testimony is veiled by complacency
Sometimes my peace of mind is swayed by doubt
Sometimes my joy is conflicted by pain
Sometimes my patience is overwhelmed by anger
Sometimes my love for others is diminished by distrust
Sometimes my hope is …

O Lord, something within me is missing
O Lord, something spiritually essential is missing
O Lord, something the saints of old sang about
Within me is missing

O Lord, what is that something
Within me that is missing

O Lord, what did grandma have
That always kept her gracefully abounding in Thy Word
What did grandma have within her heart and soul
That kept her motivated and empowered
To give generously
To serve faithfully
To love unconditionally

In addition, what did grandma have
That enabled her
To remain faithful to You
Throughout all of the changing seasons of her life
Always full of joy peace and hope

Lord, what grandma had
I also need right now
That burning desire
That something within
That never does tire
That heavenly fire
Jesus will baptize you in the Holy Ghost and fire. Matthew 3:11
You will receive power after the Holy Ghost has come upon you. Acts 1:8

O Lord, please grant me a fresh anointing
Let the power of the Holy Ghost
Fall fresh on me   Amen.

JOY WHERE ARE YOU HIDING?

Joy, Joy where are you hiding?
The night is too long!
I no longer have any more tears to shed.
How long before the morning comes?
Are you a real presence or just an ethereal dream?
Joy where are you?
Why are you avoiding me?
Unspeakable joy, where are you hiding?
Joy answered, I am here!
I have always been here, right by your side!
You could not sense my presence because you were entangled by
and listening only to your temporary discomfort and pain.
Your morning is soon coming!
Your morning is near!
Your morning is here!
Shout! Leap for Joy!
Your morning has come!

THE AGONY OF JOY

 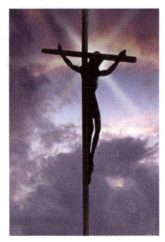

The joy that I have the world did not give it to me.
Nevertheless, the world indefatigably attempts to take it away.
My joy has transformed back into agony.
Lord, I am tired! I am weary! I am all alone!
The roads are narrowing and winding.
The hills are so steep and hard to climb.
The valleys are very deep.
The clouds are darkening and the storms are violent.
The days are too hot and the nights are so cold.
I am thirsty and hungry, and all of my muscles ache.

The criticism of people is too painful.
The disappointment, setbacks, and failures are so often.
No one is available to help me.
No one cares about me.
I am all alone.

I do not have the strength to go on.
I did not expect "favor" would be like this.
I thought "unspeakable joy" was going to be
lasting, indomitable, and different.
I did not realize that agony always surreptitiously accompanies favor.
I did not understand that God's grace, always is challenged
by life-altering tests, trials, and tribulations.
I had never experienced the agony of joy!
I am ready to throw in the towel.
I am ready to drop out of the race.
I am ready to…

Do not quit!
Do not drop out of the race!
Do not be weary!
Be encouraged!

God said, "My grace is all you need.
My power works best in weakness… 2 Corinthians 12:9

So now, be encouraged!
You can do all things through Christ, who will strengthens you!
Keep on, holding on!
The Lord is still by your side, leading, and guiding each of your footsteps.
Keep your eyes focused on Jesus Christ.
Jesus is the Conqueror who initiated, and who will sustain your faith.
Keep trusting in Jesus.
Because of the agony that was set before him.
He endured the agony of the cross at Calvary.
He endured the agony of criticism; thrust upon him by those, he came to save.
He endured the agony of sharp thorns, pressed deep into his skull.
He endured the agony of rusted nails, hammered into his hands and feet.
He endured the agony of blood, flowing profusely from his body.
He endured the agony of estrangement, being forsaken by Almighty God.

He endured the agony of evil, confronting sin, death and the grave.
Jesus Christ endured the agony disregarding the shame of the cross, just to save us.
Now, He sits in the Heavenly place of honor, at the right hand of Almighty God.

Because we are His victory, He promised, to be with us to the very end.
Because we are His victory, He promised, to enable us with unimaginable strength.
Because we are His victory, He promised, that a crown of righteousness
Awaits the faithful, who endure to the end.
Because He is The Way, The Truth, and The life ~

The agony of life culminate with unspeakable joy
for those who endure until the end.

THE UNMATACHABLE WONDER

I was blessed to have had the opportunity to behold
Several wonders of the world.

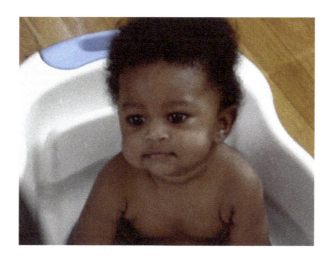

I beheld the miraculous birth of each of my children

I beheld the majestic beauty of the purple mountains

I beheld the splendor of the Grand Canyon

I beheld the awesome power of Niagara Falls

I beheld the artistic carvings on Mount Rushmore

I beheld the elegant Statue of Liberty

I beheld the monumental symbol of freedom

I beheld the unbelievable luxurious hotels of Dubai.

I beheld the phenomenal Taj Mahal

I beheld the awe-inspiring beauty of the Swiss Alps

I beheld the majestic stance of the rock of Gibraltar

I beheld the splendor of the setting sun in the African sky

I beheld the unforgettable marches on the Serengeti plains

I beheld the midnight dances of the Aurora Borealis

I beheld the cosmic eclipse of the sun

I beheld the heavenly conjunction of the planets

Each of these experience were beautiful and life inspiring
Nevertheless, there remains a spectacular wonder, a majestic glory
Which surpasses everything on earth or in this universe.
My earnest desire is to behold the Holiness of God
In all of His Glory, and to dwell in His presence forever.
I want to behold the face of Jesus Christ for myself.
I want to see Jesus!
I want to behold Jesus face to face!
The One, who bled, suffered and died on a cross for me.
I want to be in that great coronation service.
When we crown Him,
King of kings and Lord of all.
Jesus Christ is "The Unmatchable Wonder".

THE WONDER ~ ONE CAN ONLY IMAGINE

For to us, a child is born,
to us, a son is given,
and he will be called Wonderful…

Our God is awesome; there is no one like Him
In all of the universe, seen and unseen.
God always moves in majestic ways
Which are beyond the comprehension of humankind.

According to the counsel of His will,
God chose a teenager while she was still a virgin,
To carry a child miraculously conceived
In her womb by the Holy Ghost.
At the appointed time,
She was to give birth to a son,
Whom the divinely inspired prophet of antiquity
Prophesied, 400-years earlier.

The prophet obediently declared,
"He shall be called Wonderful!"
Although it did not fully express whom the Messiah is.

The birth of this infant was Wonderful!
This infant was born
During the time when the gross darkness covered the world~
Born in an odorous barn ~
Laid in an animal feeding trough~
In addition, wrapped with old strips of cloth.

One can only imagine how they felt
When, for the first time, they held him in their hands.
One can only imagine,
What a wonderment filled their soul.
Their lives had become gloriously changed.
They may have been experiencing
The unceasing peace of God,
Surpassing all corridors of understanding.
They may have been experiencing unspeakable joy
Surging through every fiber of their being.
They may have been experiencing blessed hope,
Assuring them that everything
Would be all right in the morning!

As they looked directly in the face of their newborn infant,
They were beholding the face of
God's promised Redeemer
On behalf of sinful, and estranged humanity.

One can only imagine how they may have felt
Receiving the impartation of the Holy Ghost,
Overflowing each of them with myriads of praises
To Almighty God.
One can only imagine ~ the wonder of it all!

His life as a young boy was Wonderful!
One can only imagine the excitement this couple felt

Watching their child grow and develop
Into a godly child, and respectful son.
Receiving the testimony of others about
His profound understanding of the things of God,
Surpassing the theological knowledge

And preachments of the professional religious scholars.
His parents may have been amazed
To hear him speak of his divine calling and
Intimate relationship with Jehovah God.

One can only imagine
How pleased they were
Watching their special son
Relate to their other children,
Maturing from a respectful young boy,
Into a Godly, young, wonderful man!

His life as a man was Wonderful!
At the appointed time determined by the council of God,
He moved throughout the corridors of humanity,
Fulfilling His anointed calling,
Reversing the evil acts of Satan,
Bringing forgiveness, deliverance, healing and hope,
To a broken, and lost humanity.

Jesus Christ is the Wonderful Redeemer!
God was in Christ,
reconciling the world to himself,
no longer counting people's sins against them.
2 Corinthians 5:19

There is salvation in no one else,
for there is no other name under heaven given among men
by which we must be saved.
Acts 4:12

At the name of Jesus, every knee should bow,
of things in heaven, and things in earth,
and things under the earth;
And that every tongue should confess
that Jesus Christ is Lord,
to the glory of God the Father.
Philippians 2:10

The salvific plan of The Redeemer is Wonderful!
He was wounded[a] for our transgressions,
He was [b]bruised for our iniquities;
The chastisement for our peace was upon Him,
And by His stripes[c] we are healed. Isaiah 53:5
God's divine plan for humanity is:
Incomprehensible! ~ Incapable of being deciphered
Inexplicable! ~ Unable to be explained or accounted for
Unfathomable! ~ Incapable of being fully explored or understood
Irrefragable! ~ Not able to be refuted or disproved; indisputable.
Incomparable! ~ Without equal in quality or intent
Indomitable! ~ Impossible to subdue or defeat
His name shall be called
"WONDERFUL!"

THE HIGHEST PLACE OF PRAISE AND WORSHIP

Holy, holy, holy!
Though the darkness hide thee,
Though the eye of sinful man thy glory may not see,
Only thou art holy;
There is none beside thee,
Perfect in power, in love and purity.

Holy, holy, holy!
Lord God Almighty!
All thy works shall praise thy name,
In earth and sky and sea.
Holy, holy, holy!
Merciful and mighty,
God in three persons,
Blessed Trinity.

For as the heaven is higher than earth,
so my ways are higher than your ways,
and my thoughts than your thoughts.

The Clarian call of many pastors and preachers,
Have declared and decreed,
Encouraged and admonished us to believe,
Something supernatural is about to happen!

God has predetermined,
By the sovereign counsel of His will,
To lead us to
The Highest Place of Praise and Worship.
Therefore, we must,
"Get ready! Get ready! Get ready!"

Lord, we are ready!
We are ready to do Thy holy will.
Please lead us to that Higher Place,
Which is immeasurably higher than ours is.

Lead us to that Higher Place,
Where we can authentically,
With our whole heart and soul,
Praise and worship Thee.
In spirit and in truth.

Lead us to that Place,
Where are lifted by Thy Holy Spirit,
High above the troubles of this old world.
The Place where the sounds of war
Can no longer be heard.
The Place where all sickness has been healed.
The Place where all tears are wiped away.
The Place where love covers
A multitude of our sins.

The Place where the peace of Christ abides.
The Place where joy is never-ending.
The Place where we can freely lift our hands,
Sing and shout with the heavenly host of angels,
Praises to Thy holy name.

Lord, lead us
To the Highest Place of Praise and Worship,
Where we may behold a glimpse of Thy glory.
Moreover, behold the face of our Savior,
Jesus Christ, the precious Lamb of God.
Lord, we are willing to follow,
Wherever Thy Holy Spirit will lead us.

Thus saith the Holy Spirit
My beloved children,
The Highest Place of Praise and Worship,
May not be where many people
Are naturally prone to consider.
They are primarily fixated
On their singular, earthly dimension of reality.
Moreover, their self-designated places
As being the exclusive place
For experiencing God more intimately.
Although each of their self-designated places
May have be special places
For inspiration, illumination, and blessing.

However, those places might not necessarily be,
The Highest Place of Praise and Worship.
One's bed, although a significant place
Of many blessings and healings.
Even though, it may have been there,
While they were lying down upon their bed,

I heard their unending mournful cries,
Throughout the long midnight hours.
Wiping away many of their tears.
Comforting their mind,
In addition, guarding their soul throughout the night.
Moreover, early the next morning,
Directing the morning sun to embrace them
With its majestic beams of peace and new strength,
Confirming God's promises,
"Weeping may linger awhile during the night,
Nevertheless, God's blessed gift,
The healing balm of Joy,
Comes with each new morning".
Their bed may have been
Their special place of blessings,
Nevertheless, it is not necessarily,
The Highest Place of Praise and Worship.

One's bathroom shower.
Even though, early each morning,
They might jubilantly sing,
Unaccompanied by instrumental music,
Melodious gospel songs and sacred hymns of Zion,
As each note dances its way through
Every droplet of water,
Washing away, the physical impurities
Of the day or night past.
Even though the shower room
Might be a daily place of physical cleansing and rejuvenation.
The shower room is not necessarily,
The Highest Place of Praise and Worship.

Rising early each morning,
Sitting down at the kitchen table.

The bible, notes and other devotional materials,
Are spread out around the table.
Reading, studying, and meditating.
Although it might be your special place,
For your daily ritual.
That special place where you prepare yourself
To meet the challenges for the new day.
It may not, necessarily be,
The Highest Place of Praise and Worship.

That place in your home,
Your secret closet,
Your "war room"
The place, which you have chosen to
Contend with Satan and his demons.
The place where you attempt
To tear down strongholds,
The place where you prayed,
To cover your family and loved ones.
Even there, where you have claimed
So many victories,
Moreover, it may not necessarily be,
The Highest Place of Praise and Worship.

For the most part, many have the privilege
To have their own vehicle to travel
Along the dangerous highways,
To their varied destinations.
Some have designated their vehicle,
And their times of traveling along the highways and byways
As their special place of inspiration and joy.
Where they can join in singing,
Uninhibitedly, along with
Their favorite gospel-recording artist.

Sometimes, unrestrained tears of joy
Stream down the sides of their face,
Sometime, they feel compelled
To pull over to the side of the road.

Although their designated places may be daily transitional spaces
Of inspiration and unexpected joy,
They may not necessarily be,
The Highest Place of Praise and Worship.

Traditionally, congregants gather on Sundays
In addition, at other times of the week to worship.
Some congregants have designated a seat on the aisle,
That is their exclusive space.
Declaring it to others, "That's my seat".
Even though, seated and standing in their respective spaces,
Singing the songs of Zion,
Listening to bible readings,
Listening to or reciting prayers,
Listening to sermons or homilies,
The place where they are gathered,
May not necessarily be,
The Highest Place of Praise.

If one where to climb the highest mountains
In the world,
Beholding the beauty of creation,
Declaring its majesty and magnificence,
Mount Everest in Asia~ 29,029 feet
Aconcagua in South America~ 22,838 feet
Mount McKinley in North America~ 20,322 feet
Mount Elbrus in Europe/Asia~ 18,510 feet
Mount Blanc in Europe~ 15,780 feet
Mount Kirkpatrick in Antarctica~ 14,856 feet

Mount Kosciuszko in Australia ~7,310 feet
Those glorious places of God's creation,
May not necessarily be,
The Highest places of Praise and Worship
Although, each of the designated place chosen by man
May hold a special place in the heart
For encouragement, inspiration, joy and amazement.
Each of those places,
If absent of authentic faith,
And the anointing of the Holy Spirit,
Can merely become places of religiosity,
Or places where forms of praise and worship
Are ritual practices,
But, without the essential manifestation
Of the presence of the Holy Spirit,
Which is humility and authentic faith.

The Highest Place of Praise and Worship is not a physical place.
The Highest Place is the most glorious place.
The place of spiritual humility.
The example has been displayed throughout the biblical,
Moreover, throughout all of the stages of human history.
The cherubim and seraphim
Day and night they never stop saying:" 'Holy, holy, holy
is the Lord God Almighty, who was, and is, and is to come."
Holy, Holy, Holy
The twenty-four Elders seated around the throne of God,
Bow down before Almighty God.
As they worship God,
They lay their crowns before His throne and say:
You are worthy, our Lord and God,
to receive glory and honor and power,
for you created all things,

and by your will, they were created
and have their being.   Revelation 4:11

Moreover, the day is rapidly approaching when
What John, the apostolic prophet
Clearly articulated will soon come to fruition.
Every creature which is in heaven,
and on the earth, and under the earth,
and such as are in the sea, and all that are in them,
heard I saying,
Blessing, and honor, and glory, and power,
unto him that sitteth upon the throne,
and unto the Lamb for ever and ever.
Revelation 5:13

Additionally, God has given Jesus Christ a name that is above every name:
God elevated him to the place of highest honor
and gave him the name above all other names,
that at the name of Jesus every knee should bow,
in heaven and on earth and under the earth,
and every tongue confess that Jesus Christ is Lord,
to the glory of God the Father.
Philippians 2:10

The Highest Place of Praise and Worship,
Is kneeling in the presence of God
Upon bended knees,
With a heart filled with authentic faith,
Humility and adoration.

The God whom we serve is
Omnipotent, Omniscient and Omnipresent.
God will transform,

Any place on Earth,
Into a sacred place,
Of pure praise and worship,
If anyone honestly, and humbly yields
To the indwelling presence of the Holy Spirit.
In addition, follows His leading,
Walking under the covering of His anointing.

Thus saith the Holy Spirit,
The Highest Place of Praise and Worship
Is the most spiritually humble place.
On bended knees,
Before the holy presence of Almighty God.

I STAND AMAZED

My soul sings, O Lord,
How excellent is Thy name throughout the entire universe!

O Lord, how majestic and glorious is Thy name
Throughout the entire cosmos,
Seen and unseen!
When I think about the magnificent works of Thy hands
In particular, the formation of humankind,
As the apex of Thy Creation;

When I attempt to grasp the unimaginable,
Which, by divine intentionality,
You sovereignly created us in Your image
I Stand Amazed!

When I examine the structure of the human brain
Which contains trillions of synchronistic synapses
Interacting with billions of neutrons,

Providing humans with the capacity,
Too instantly, communicate,
And then to transmigrate simultaneously,

The natural and supernatural dimensions of the universe,
I Stand Amazed!

My soul sings, O Lord, how great Thou art!
When I realize that,
Good health is vital to our continued existence,
When I feel the invisible, continuous soft beats of my heart,
Conjoined with the myriad of dynamic thoughts
That traverse through my mind,
When I understand that,
The heart is the hiding place
Of my exclusive comfort zone;

The seat of my
Emotions, intentions, and passions.
The sacred place,
Where God has chosen to abide ~
I Stand Amazed!

My soul sings and shouts, "Glory' glory, glory!"
When I accept the fact that You sent Jesus to Earth
To save all sinners just like me!
He suffered, bled and died
At Calvary, to redeem a wretch like me.
In three days He rose from the grave,
Conquering sin, death and the grave
To save a sin sick soul like mine.
Whose precious blood washed and made me completely whole
I Stand Amazed!

God did it all, just for you and me!
His love for us is beyond comprehension!
I Stand Amazed!

TO GOD BE THE GLORY!

CPSIA information can be obtained
at www.ICGtesting.com
Printed in the USA
JSHW021054080520
5571JS00002B/3